To Save A Daughter

How we decided to stop the traffickers...
...before they got the girls!

Ken Harbour

A book by:
The Transformation Fellowship

Published by Get Out Of the Box Publishing
Forest, Va.

http://www.savethedaughters.com

ISBN-13:978-0692737606

Table of Contents

How To Use This Book

    To begin, this is not a large book, and it's not intended to be. It was written and formatted so you could read it quickly. I'll tell you why I'm penning it in a few moments, but here's how you should approach it. Explore the words with reality in mind! And when I say reality, I mean try to imagine that the stories you are reading are real, because in fact, for almost this entire book, they are. Each short chapter comes from either a person or persons familiar to us or a combination of a couple of people and places that happened in the course of our ministry. The facts are real. The places are real. The smells, the pain, and the events are real. Most of all, the dangers to young girls in Nepal, and their potential trafficking into India, is very real. Save the Daughters, is a project of our 501(c) (3) organization. We believe we discovered a way to radically prevent and deter the abuse happening in the Himalayas and offer young girls a message of hope at the same time. After a few short years, we have become the premier organization that actually PREVENTS trafficking in that country, warning as many as 25,000 young village girls and families a year. At the end of the pages you will have an opportunity to make a decision. Will you join us in making a difference and saving just one daughter? I hope you will. The smallest gift can have immeasurable impact. But most of all, I hope you are able to enjoy knowing that in the midst of all the nasty that's in the world, there is one Christian organization making a difference. Someone is saving daughters. Read slowly...the daughters would want you to.

Why I'm Writing This Book

In my thirty years of missionary experience, particularly working within emerging groups referred to as third-world, I've seen the good and the bad. I've seen the groups and organizations that are full of integrity, and I've seen those trading upon whomever they can for a dollar donation. I've watched sensitive Western mission groups traveling abroad do good, and I've seen others, less sensitive, create incredible harm and damage. <u>We have learned how to partner with, cultivate, and see to the finish, strategically implemented projects that are nothing short of transformational</u>. We've become experts in the unique. We have one major goal: To bear fruit...and that it should remain forever.

When we started this project, figures stated that each year, between 7,500 and 14,000 Nepali girls were being lured into the brothels of India. After getting it up and running and seeing it grow into a mature ministry project, we can proudly say that upwards of 25,000 young girls and boys are educated about the dangers and warned each year. Those in high risk areas along the border of Nepal and India, in the rural villages, and in the very school yards where traffickers come to deceive...our teams are making an eternal difference. This short book is about how it came about, and what the context is for those working in, falling captive to, or escaping from the tragedy that is literally a hell on earth. **I'm writing this for the daughters** to inform you and, quite frankly, in the hope you will join our cause in a ministry that works. Join a ministry where you will know your gifts create lasting and positive change.

But most of all, I'm writing this for the daughters.

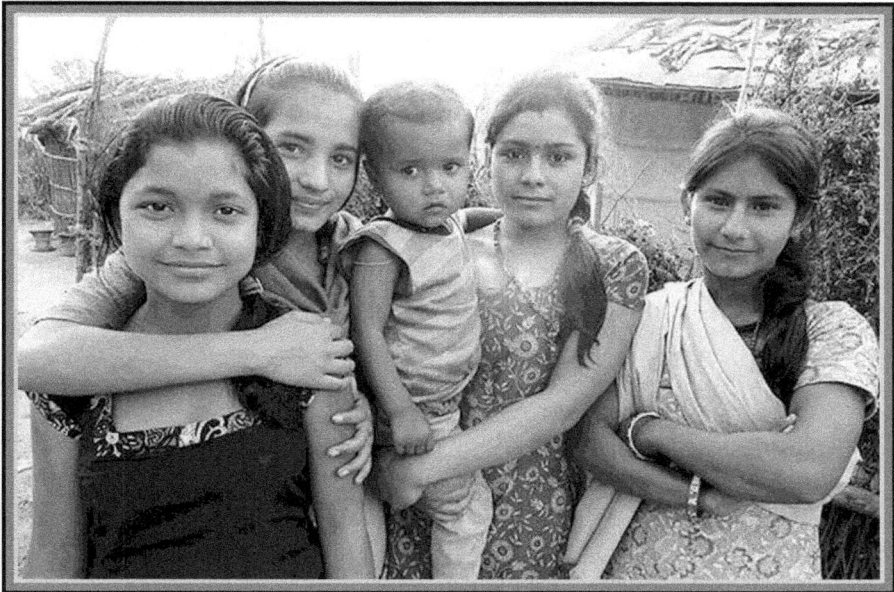

The Woman

Between 7,500 and 14,000 young Nepali girls are trafficked into India every year for sexual exploitation and forced prostitution.

It was Saturday, and I sat on the floor of the humble church building with the rest of the crowd doing my best to create a comfortable spot to rest for the next two or more hours. The concrete floor was covered with a few bamboo mats, but they did little to actually pad the concrete. And although I had become accustomed to sitting in the Asian fashion, my American tail bones still weren't happy. We were watching the Nepali children sing. It always makes me happy to the core when watching them because they sing with such abandon and joy. Many just close their eyes, with their little faces lifted upward, and I always say something like this to myself, "I've never seen American kids sing like that in church." Take my word for it, it's truly beautiful and must gather much heavenly attention. I know it sounds strange to say church on Saturday, but that's when most of the Christians in this country have the opportunity since it's a day off for Hindus, and Sunday is a work day. Cultures are different everywhere, aren't they?

4

I was dog tired. And I mean physically spent. I was young, full of zeal, reasonably healthy, but I was on the last week of a six-week trip and had spent the better part of the past nine days out in the mountains visiting small Christian groups teaching, encouraging, and doing my best not to get sick. Those days were filled with climbing the ridges and steep paths that made their way through the Himalayan outback to village after village. The nights were filled with singing, sharing of meager meals, long talks around an oil lamp, and then a questionable night's sleep in a sleeping bag on the floor hoping that no unfriendly insect or reptile would find my warmth attractive. Now I was glad to be back in Kathmandu, and the guest house I was staying in was only costing me $2 a night. Great deal!

It wasn't a Sheraton, but thank you God it was a place where water was both safe and fresh, and where I could get some decent, clean food with a clean sheet to sleep on. But I was still tired.

Three years earlier I had helped send a young man named Santé to the outskirts of Kathmandu to begin work in the Harasiddhi region. There was a massive brick factory located there and most of the people who were employed in the grueling daily effort to make the bricks came from low caste groups. These poor people would work from dawn to dusk with little hope of advancement in this life, laboring for just enough food to keep the family going another week. Sending one of their children to school was unheard of since many of the children worked right alongside the parents.

I had watched young Santé grow from a teenager into a young man full of fire and zeal. It wasn't unusual to find him riding the streets of Kathmandu late at night coming home on his bicycle from a Bible study he was conducting for a group of poor believers or seekers. He had heart. I had slowly encouraged his work, and it was bearing fruit. Now he was a full-fledged church planter, and he was serving among a group of people few wanted to serve: the poor, disenfranchised, and despised. It took him about two years, but he had grown the little fellowship to nearly a hundred men and women. Quite a feat that was accomplished in such a short time. And in the little brick, mud, and bamboo house where we were conducting a church service, the noise, the smells, and the loud praise were all mixed together. There are few things that will transport you back into early church times like going to a house church in Nepal; especially in the early years.

I had been introduced to those assembled, and I started sharing with the help of a translator. I understood Nepali and

Hindi fairly well. Both share the same linguistic roots as Urdu, the language that developed in the conquering Alexander the Great's military camp so that the different warriors could speak to one another. That language was structured just like the Greek of Alexander, and since I had been an ancient language Greek major in college, it was much easier for me to imbibe the other languages.

However, the West Virginia accent that I'd grown up with sabotaged any valid attempt to communicate like a native in this country, so I wisely utilized a translator when teaching. My eyes were going back and forth over the crowd like one of those old fans you would see in a room that slowly blew left then right. All were sitting on the floor in front of me as I preached, the men on one side and women on the opposite, as was the Nepali custom. I was watching their faces, catching their eyes as I tried my best to animate the story I was telling. I scanned across the women's faces again and that's when I saw her.... "THE WOMAN."

I don't think I can even describe the look accurately, but if ever grief could be seen, there it hung around her neck like a massive chain. Her eyes were dark yet visibly scared. Her countenance was pallid, and as I continued to look at her, it was as if she were the only woman sitting on the floor but sitting in a shadow. Things like this would happen to me when ministering in Asia in the early years, and I know it might sound bizarre to you, but all I will say is that many times God seemed to show me things that needed attention when I was traveling or ministering. I'd get a strong impression; see a word in my mind, or something. If I were in a place of oppression, the feeling was viscous. If a person needed to be specifically encouraged, words would come to me that many times only made sense to the individual in need. It's really difficult to explain, and I don't want to set a theological precept down, but without a doubt, this lady had a spirit of despair all over her and I knew it...**then and there!!**

So I paused and turned to the Nepali brother translating and asked him to interpret for me as I walked closer to her. I stepped around and through the women and girls sitting on the floor and stood about three feet from the lady. I looked as deeply into her eyes and spirit as I could, silently praying to myself. I asked her name, and she bowed her head just a bit, softly mumbling a name I couldn't make out. The room fell silent as I told the brother to tell this sister that the Lord had shown me a shadow of despair around her face and body.

This was a hard thing to do in the American church, but here I was calling out this sister in a little building a world away from my hometown. I was so certain of what I was seeing. There was a very long silence as her shoulders bent and started to shake....everyone was looking at her...then she burst into tears! She was literally crying so hard she had to hold herself up by leaning on one of the ladies next to her. Something was about to happen!

The room was deadly still and some women were holding their children tight so they wouldn't make noise. Another lady sitting on the other side of the woman put a hand on her shoulder and started praying. The woman was trying to say something through the sobbing, but it was quite unintelligible to me. Through coaxing and gentle words from the translator, she finally started quieting down and began to speak. Her 14-year-old daughter had been missing for two days, and she was afraid that she had been stolen or kidnapped into the bordering area with India to be sold as a prostitute. I knew God hadn't shown me this just to impress anyone or get a rise of amazement from people, so I asked the teary-eyed sister if the authorities had been informed. She said, "No." I instructed the other ladies of the fellowship to "intercede to God" on behalf of this sister and ask specifically that the daughter might be found. Now when a group of Nepali women pray, they really pray.

There's nothing like a mother's heart to open the gates of glory. Many gathered around this crushed sister praying and crying as I turned to the translator on my right.

We decided to stop the service, leaving young Santé to oversee the women as they attended the distraught mother. Then another leading brother from our team left to find a telephone to send a message to his brother, a high level police officer in Kathmandu. If anything could be done through the police to find the young girl, he was certain his brother, who was sympathetic to the Christian minority in the country, would help.

Four days passed, and I was to leave the next day for my 35-hour trip home. I was visiting at the house of our country coordinator, discussing ministry goals for the year, drinking copious amounts of Nepali tea, and saying my goodbyes when a messenger came to the door. The messenger had been sent from the Nepali brother whose family member was a policeman. **The young girl had been found on the border of Nepal awaiting sale into India**.

She had been rescued before crossing the border and was being returned to her family untouched. The ones responsible for taking her had escaped, but they thought they knew who they were and were still trying to catch them. Everyone sharing tea that morning immediately started talking about the event and telling the leader serving us tea about the church service on Saturday...how events happened.....me stopping the service....and how the lady responded with tears and fear. As they talked, I looked into my tea and stirred it very slowly, my heart churning with emotion. Nobody knew at that time that I was doing my very best not to tear up. The knot came up into my throat so quickly, and my heart was experiencing a strange mixture of relief and fear.

I remember vividly thinking about my own daughter some 7,700 miles away. What if that had been my little girl? What if she had been taken? The tears were visible now running down my cheeks, and my coordinator stood up and started thanking God for the girl's safe return which prompted the whole room to break out in a crescendo of praise. I let my own words mix with theirs and dried the tears from my face as we all broke into a song.

This was the first time I'd ever heard about the trafficking in Nepal.

The year was 1994......the woman's despair has never left my memory.

The seed was planted!

Simple Church in Nepal

A typical village kitchen

The Strategy

"What's the use of running if you are not on the right road?" — German proverb

It was late in the afternoon in the fall of 2009, and I was sitting in the Teleju restaurant with my feet on the opposite chair trying to relax after a stressful day. I was waiting patiently for the Himalayan Mountain Range to catch the evening sun and shout in my face "See this"…"Don't forget it"… The wind was coming from west to east as usual across the range, and from where we were in the valley it looked like small puffs of fresh smoke being caught by a breeze and carried away. I had discovered this little hideaway years ago on one of my earlier trips back in 1992.

This restaurant is located on the southern side of Kathmandu in Patan Square. Patan Square is a very important stopover for tourists visiting Nepal. I usually avoid these places, but the vantage point on the fourth floor of this small building was too much for me to miss. Besides, I could make journal notes and think through things here rather than some exhaust and dust-filled restaurant on a lower street level. Patan was founded somewhere around the 3rd century B.C. The area where it is located, Latitpur, is one of the oldest in Kathmandu dating back to

13

around 299 A.D. Some of the world's oldest temples are in this place, and it's special to both Hindus and Buddhists. From my vantage point I could watch the street hawkers trying to convince tourists from Europe, Japan, Ukraine, and other places that their souvenirs were original and very costly. Boy, it had surely changed from my earlier days in the mountains.

My attention returned to the peaks as the setting sun began to drape the mountains in a spectacular lavender hue. Regardless of the beauty, my mind was occupied with the problem I was dealing with. We had started helping select NGO's (Non-Governmental Organizations) with their border-watch stations that were located at crucial places along the border of Nepal, but after a year and a half of serious research, the same phrase was slapping me right in the face, **"This isn't solving the problem, Ken."** Now don't get me wrong, it was working, but not that well. It wasn't that effective. That's when I remembered the conversation I had with an engineer years ago that had made such an impression.

He was a very successful engineer who constructed commercial properties, and I had a relationship with him as a donor for ministry and project efforts in various countries. I was having a phone conversation long distance one afternoon discussing problems in an organization we both knew about; when he said something I've never forgotten. He said, "Ken, engineers want to know how to fix the problem and good ones want to know how to fix it so it doesn't happen again." That made so much sense to me and I've never forgotten it. And that's when my mind kicked into my medical background. Bear with me a bit as you read this!

You see, my wife and I are Board Certified Acupuncturists. We spent a lot of time in Asia and decided at a point in our lives that natural medicine, which we call "creation-based", is a very effective option. We learned this from our friends in Asia, many of whom were Christian medical doctors. Though they had been through rigorous medical training, they knew the time-tested value of the cultural medicine they grew up with and practiced it alongside their Western style. When my wife and I went through our four-year program to obtain our medical credentials, one of the things we were taught in order to deal effectively with a chronic disease or ailment someone was experiencing was that you have to make sure you are accomplishing at least one thing in particularly. **You have to get to the "root of the problem**." You just couldn't continue to mask the symptoms because what was causing the sickness was the real issue……"find the root." That's where the fix lies…at the root. Don't treat the symptom if you can fix the root.

So here I am sitting in one of the most beautiful, and little-discovered spots in the world with my eyes moving from beautiful mountains to tourists far below, back and forth while I silently whispered to myself....how do we get to the root of this thing? How do we fix it so it doesn't keep happening?

I can't really say the skies opened and there was a choir playing, but I can tell you for certain that I stood up and walked slowly over to the concrete parapet. Here's what I said to myself: "If the main problem is that they are deceiving unsuspecting village girls, then our task is to either stop the deceiver or expose the deceiver. The main problem is that the families and the girls want an opportunity, but they aren't being told the truth. We have to expose the liars!"

And I made the decision that day. We would see if we could find a way to go to the mountain and border villages and teach both the literate and the illiterate about the dangers awaiting them and the life of hell and torment for those who were deceived. We would work with the village leaders, and we would look young girls and their parents in their eyes and educate. We would take the opportunity to tell them that daughters were just

16

as important as sons. Everything had just changed in those few moments. And it's a measure of pride for me to say that within six months of that day, we would have our first team of seven trained personnel traveling to a high-trafficking area along the border of Nepal and India for over two weeks of village education and open air meetings. Within three years of this day we would have effectively warned nearly 45,000 young people and their families. <u>We had found a key to stopping the trafficking and providing an opening for the Good News</u>! Save The Daughters is now making an incredible impact!

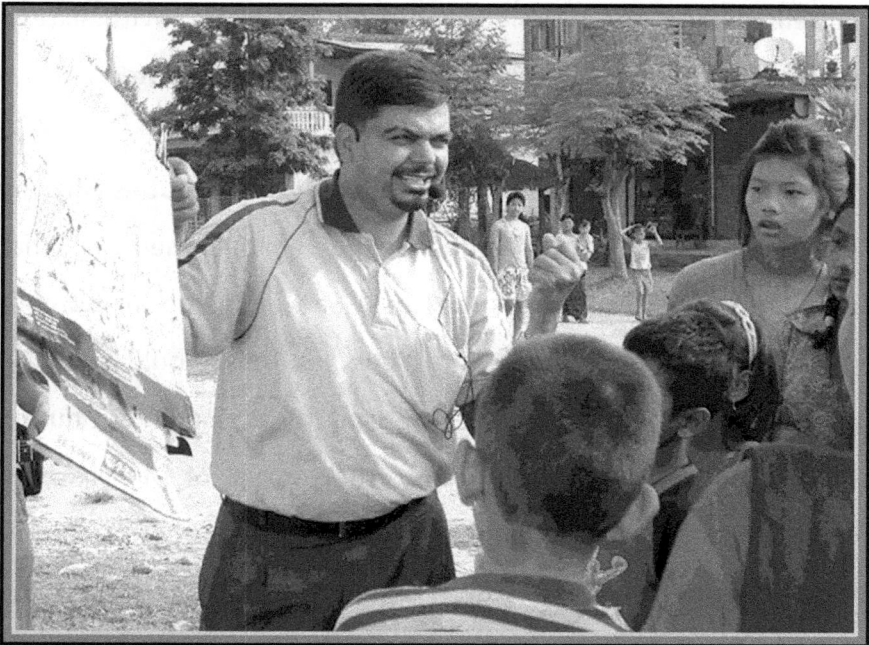

Sharing an anti-trafficking message in the context of hope

Sundari - A Daughter Lost

My parents named me Sundari which means beautiful,
but now I am called Amoli (Priceless). But that lasted a short time
until the men decided I wasn't.

I awoke early with the smell of the last client still clinging to my body like a sari after a rain, except the rain makes you feel clean and its smell reminds you of life and home. I sat on the edge of my bed for a moment to gather my thoughts before trudging off to the private room at the end of the hall to relieve myself. It was not occupied, and I felt fortunate. With sixteen girls in the building, this room was often the most coveted.

I walked back to my room mindful of the duties that lay ahead of me before the afternoon came. I had learned early that during the religious holidays the house saw an increasing number of clients coming to "offer sacrifices" as they would say. To accommodate only seven was a blessing for my body. But during these times, and especially during the festival of Diwali, there could be as many as nineteen, even though the house-mother raised the prices 200 Rupees.

I walked back into the room which I shared during the day

with two other girls and stood at the window for just a moment. It was the smell of rice fields in the early morning I sought, but I knew deep inside that the five-story building in front of me would be my only view. If I could only see the mountains again. The building was dark and gray and looked as if the sun had never cleansed it of the lingering darkness that invaded all the spaces.

I walked to my bed and reached under the mattress as far as I could, making sure I was alone in the room. I took out the small, woven piece of cloth that I'd saved when the house-mother took my mountain clothes away to sell to others on the day my dreams died. It was tucked into the corner of the mattress where it could not be found. I looked down at the torn patch from what had been my best dress. It brought a brief moment of light followed by crushing reality, today was my 15th birthday. I'd been here for almost three years.

I still remember when the agents came to my village three years ago. My life began in a place near Sano Dumma in the hill section of east Nepal. My family was very proud because we were Newar people, the original rulers of Nepal, and of higher importance than other castes. All the village people said I was beautiful and smart. That was me, Sundari, the smart one, and yes, they said I was beautiful.

The two men were brothers and yet were very different in their language. They said they represented agents in Dharan who had educational job offerings in India. They often spoke in Hindi rather than our superior Newari language. But their story was a dream come true. Everyone became very excited, and our mothers did their best to make us look as exceptional as possible. We even took time to memorize things about our desires for advancement and life so these men would choose us. ONLY THREE WOULD GET THE OPPORTUNITY! If only we had known!

After two quick days, I stood out above all the girls. My father and mother were so proud. There were two other girls, but I knew if it came to a contest, I would beat them. My parents were paid a very large amount of money, nearly $200. I glowed with pride. Finally, my father would smile when people talked about me. A portion was given to the Village Chairman who had allowed the contest, but I didn't care. I was going to learn how to serve in a very important business and receive more education than any in our simple village school could imagine. I can still see the faces of the girls I went to school with as they watched us depart down the mountain. I held my head high as we left the village. If only someone had warned us.

Down the great river road to the Barahcherea Temple we

went. It took two full days. From there we were put on an overnight speed bus to Dharan. I'd heard of the large Eastern Nepali City, but was so disappointed to stop only for a few moments to change buses. The two brothers now were joined by a woman that they said was their sister. She went with us as we relieved ourselves and sought rice and tea to warm our bodies.

I thought we would have to show our village papers at the border, but when the bus stopped just south of Biratnagar for the Indian Border crossing, one of the brothers began to talk to a border guard who quickly put us back onto the bus while taking a number of rupees and putting them into his coat pocket. After that it was just a very long trip. I remember arriving at the rail station and getting second class tickets. Yes, we were important. It was true. We were traveling second class.

The trip south began. I still remember the town names: Araria, Raiganj, Kaliachak, and even one called English Bazar. How strange. The British had left their mark on everything...even names of towns. As we approached Kolkata my excitement couldn't be contained. Would I be taught to work in an office? Would I serve a dignitary or a politician? Perhaps I would learn to watch over the children of wealthy business families. I grew more anxious to arrive. After two days of rail and station names I can't

21

bring to mind, we arrived at a place called Howrah Rail Station.

The two brothers had become increasingly irritable. If we talked too much or asked too many questions, they became angry and told us there were final arrangements to be made. And as mountain girls from Nepal, we should know to keep silent and let them conduct their business properly. I was quick to submit. I wanted the best position. I knew I would win!

While we loaded our small bags into the single taxi, I asked the oldest brother how long it would take to get to the employment office. My stomach was feeling uncomfortable with the food we had gotten on the rail, and I hoped it wasn't so far. "Less than 85 kilometers," he said. I grew hopeful. I would reach my dream within a few hours.

I'd never experienced anything like Kolkata. Known as Calcutta to most of the world, I'd later learn that the city had nearly four and one-half million people. In less than four minutes I was lost. But the taxi kept going along a river following what seemed to be a very traveled route. We passed primary schools, a few parks, houses all in a row that looked new and important. I was happy but couldn't fight the sleep that demanded attention and slowly closed my eyes for just a moment. The quick stopping of the taxi jerked me back to life, and I rubbed my eyes with anticipation.

This didn't look like a wealthy area. Everything around us appeared as one of the market areas in the larger towns we'd passed through coming here, except the buildings were at least four or five sections high. Everything looked old and you could tell by the air coming through the taxi window that it had been a long time since anything fresh had found its way here. The gutter just outside the taxi window smelled like a long forgotten toilet, and the exhaust from the thousands of motorbikes hung low in the air. It was oppressive!

We hadn't heard the negotiations that took place between the house-mother and the two agents who brought us from the mountains, but we later found out we were sold for $900 each. The brothers told us that the employment people would process us within and I, along with the other two mountain girls, walked inside with hesitancy hoping that a mistake had been made.

The first night turned into tears.

The second night turned into a living nightmare. Then the beatings followed. I was tied to a bed so I wouldn't escape. Girls who had been there before me came into my room and urged me to submit to the reality.

The third night I was sold to a high paying client for $137. He was told that a virgin could take away his AIDS symptoms. I just remember the pain that night and again with the three others who came the next night. I was twelve years old and now part of the 11,000 prostitutes in Sonaganchi Red Light District, the oldest in Kolkata.

I held the patch of cloth tightly in my fingers and closed my eyes hoping the pressure would somehow bring the high mountains of the Koshi Range into view again. If I squeezed enough, I could hear my mother's voice...smell morning tea and rice boiling. If I just held it long enough, perhaps everything could change for just a moment. But it didn't. The overcooked rice from the vendor down the street coupled with day-old fried samosa was my only reward. Instead of crisp mountain air, I had kerosene, stale cigarette smoke, and indescribable street filth creeping though the bars on the window. Instead of the soft hum of village life and the occasional sound of goats, there was the blaring of horns and battling rickshaws and motorcycles.

I closed the curtain. I listened to the sounds in the busy

street, knowing that someone would call my name soon. They would say "Amoli (Priceless), come!" Would I ever be Sundari again? Why hadn't we known?

Little mountain girls

Village girls who are at risk

Rhohita - Of The Dhading Hills

Rohita walked slowly across the center of the village to the stall where she sold tea. The fire was burning intensely atop the stone fireplace in front of the house and gave off welcome warmth. The crude sign hanging just above the stall said GOOD FOOD, but she was old enough to know that it was only a slogan to entice trekkers into a momentary pause on their way into the Gamesh Himal. This section of the Himalaya Range was a favorite for tourists with its towering peaks and the swift waters of the Bagmati River. The combination of trekking and white-water rafting had become a source of extra income for all residents of the sacred Hindu mountains The sign had worked many times before, and whenever a tourist would stop for tea, she might be rewarded with a piece of candy. Sometimes, if she was very careful, she could even hide these treats from the man and woman she was living with and have it all for herself and her brothers and sisters.

She was only nine when she started washing dishes in the village. She was grateful for the small place she was able to share with her four siblings. At least they had a roof over their heads and blankets for warmth. But after three years of working, the

Village Committee Leader had become more demanding and she had no idea what the future might have in store for her or her two brothers and two sisters. She put the water where it was supposed to be set, just as the neighbor who cooked the rice had demanded it. Pausing for a moment, Rhohita looked up into the mountains taking a liberal breath of air and stretched her sore arms. Was there ever a more beautiful place, she thought to herself.

It was one of the few locations in the world where you could view the mountains rising before your eyes without obstruction. The first Kings of Nepal had created their Kingdoms here allowing the area's majesty and natural fortress-like surroundings to proclaim their nobility. But Rhohita knew very little of those facts from the history of her country. She only knew she was from the place of the Kings and seeing foreigners made her feel special.

That was why so many trekkers came through the area. The beauty and grandeur were unparalleled. They would stand in awe of the mountains and take picture after picture of the snow clad peaks that reached into the clouds. Sometimes they would snap a picture of a village hut or even take a moment to smile at her with their unusual faces. Occasionally, one would get that look in their eye and she would silently know that the possibility of being offered a chocolate or a few rupees would come next. Rupees always attracted the wife of the Committee Leader quickly, and Rhohita thought she must be able to smell the money like the mouse that always managed to find the bread crumbs around the bottom of the tea stall every night. She always took the money from Rhohita.

When her father was alive, she could remember sitting on his knee as he pointed out the route he would take, proudly carrying supplies from one village district to another. She would follow his words as he pointed to the furthest peak. Then he would lift her on his shoulders so she could see it better. She was so proud of her father. He was strong and in her young mind seemed special among all the other men in the village. Their family had come from a long history of mountain porters, and her father was very strong.

However, the truth of the matter was hidden from her. The family was from a lower caste and if it wasn't for their ability to walk and carry great loads toiling across the treacherous mountain paths weekly, there would be no work. Her father's work was incredibly dangerous, but she was young and unaware of these things.

Time came to a standstill when one such path proved too dangerous on a winter day. News came to their simple mud and wood hut that he had been killed in an accident high on the mountain. The body was lost in the river below. Her mother was silent for many days. The joy had left their lives.

Unfortunately, it was Rhohita who found her mother nine days after the prescribed mourning period was over. She had decided to follow her husband, the love of her life, into death and not face the prospect of raising five children alone at her age in the vast rural region. Rhohita was now head of the family.

But things seemed to change in April of the year when the Village Committee Leader and his wife received the visitors from Kathmandu. The visitors were very important. They were called Mr. and Mrs. Tamang and they had been in the village for three days going from one place to the other, spreading informational pamphlets which she couldn't read nor cared to try. She knew two things, first, they were important, and second, she was just glad that the wife of the Village Leader was occupied with someone other than her. Rhohita had even managed to get a whole candy bar from a lady trekker and that night all of her brothers and sisters were as quiet as possible as she broke off pieces for each of them.

On the fourth evening, the Leader and his wife had the visitors in their small hut and required Rhohita to serve them tea and soup. The visiting couple said they were very pleased at her manner, and left some new clothes for her as a gift as they praised her. They also left gifts for the Village Committee Leader and his wife which made such an impression on the VC's wife, that she showed everyone she could and didn't hesitate to make sure they all knew how important she and her husband were.

Rhohita couldn't believe her luck as she shared the story with her brothers and sisters. She had been singled out and given complements by the strangers along with new clothes. Her little sister Sunari was overjoyed, but the oldest brother, Biswas, kept asking if anyone was going to give him a gift. She smiled thinking the future was going to be brighter. And it did get brighter the very next day.

The VC leader and his wife told her that she was to leave within two days and go with the strangers where they would arrange for a position of employment and education. They were so impressed with her that they had decided to use their influence to gain her an important position. Rhohita was living a dream come true.

Little did this precious unsuspecting mountain girl ever think that the couple was involved in acquiring the innocent mountain girls like herself, and selling them to traffickers who, in turn, would smuggle them across the border to be sold into the Indian brothels. The dream would become a nightmare.

The morning they were to leave, Rhohita was returning from gathering her last water pot filled from the tube pipe that descended from the spring above. The tube pipe ran almost 1000 meters from the largest spring at the top of the hill. Climbing every morning without stopping, it would take her an hour just to carry three pots of water down to the village. People of her caste weren't allowed to use the well in the village, so she was grateful that two years ago, government people came from Kathmandu to the area to run the pipe from the clean water above. Rhohita had waited patiently that morning as the older women all saw to the filling of their water pots and then she had to wait for the older girls to get water. It was a tradition repeated every day, but she had to wait patiently or she would receive more than just a sharp rebuke. But today was different, and she smiled as she put the last pot down; soon, she would never have to do this again.

As she walked down the hillside, getting closer to the side of the hut owned by the Village Committee Leader, she heard loud voices. She slowed, her feet moving forward ever so softly. Perhaps someone had changed their mind. Was there a fight? Did the visitors decided against taking her, or did the wife decide she was needed at the tea stall?   Her mind reeled in space, searching every avenue of explanation.   Perhaps she had left the rice boiling and there was a problem serving the guests.   Her mind raced through the possible problems she might have caused and then she stopped to listen closer.

Apparently the argument was about her worth and the….the…the… **MONEY TO BE PAID FOR HER**. She froze. It didn't take her long, listening to the conversation, to understand that the Village Committee Leader and his wife were selling her. Selling her! To whom? Selling her! For how much? They didn't have this right! She did not belong to anyone but her dead father and mother. The longer she listened the more fearful she became. The couple from Kathmandu had offered $350, but the Village Committee Leader and his wife wanted $450. Besides, they had reasoned to themselves, there were two more sisters, let's see how much we can get for this one.

Stepping ever so lightly around the water pot, she turned and began running. She slowed down as she came closer to other houses where people were starting their day, but as soon as she was safely past, she began running across the mountain path that led to the terraced hills to the west. When she finally ran out of breath, she stopped and began to cry uncontrollably. The crying became sobs as she thought about being separated from her brothers and sisters forever. She was to be sold like an animal! But what could she do? Why had her father had to die? Why had her mother left her children when such awful things could happen? Where could she hide?

She sat on the side of the hill for what seemed to be forever, her little arms locked tightly around her knees. Occasionally, she would look around to check for pursuers. She kept thinking to herself over and over, "Where can I hide? Where will I be safe?" Her eyes scanned the crest of the path from where she had come, making sure no one was looking for her. Then her eyes searched the hills desperately looking for a sign of hope. At the last moment, when desperation screamed that no hope would be found, the village of Tinpiple came into view from the farthest valley below. A picture sprang into her memory of a man and wife who had shown her kindness several times. He was known to be a Christian Pastor in the mountains, and the village leaders had strictly instructed all the children to avoid them. But Rhohita remembered the times before, early in the morning, when the Pastor stopped at the tea stall on his way to visit other

Christians in the area. He had a very kind voice and his face and eyes would light up when he spoke. He never treated her like a low caste girl either. She remembered saying to herself, "How can this man be so bad?"

She found her feet, and soon the adrenalin pumping through her little body propelled her down the terraced rice fields like a goat running from a leopard. Down she went! Scurrying effortlessly around large rocks and jumping ditches, she navigated the twisting path with the skill of a genuine mountain girl. She did not stop until she came to the village of Tinpiple 3000 feet below.

Rhohita asked each person she approached where she could find Pastor Mahesh. "Where is Pastor?" she would say. Over and over and over. "Where is Pastor? Where is Pastor?" She had turned to start down to the next village when she felt a hand on her shoulder. She turned in fear thinking it was the visitor from Kathmandu, only to see the big kind eyes of Pastor Mahesh Tamang looking down at her with curiosity. "Little one," he said, "slow down. You are far from your home. Are you alright?"

To this day she can't remember why she grabbed at his side and began crying again, but she did. It had been so long since her father had died, and when the pastor held her little shaking body a memory surfaced from a long forgotten place in her heart. She felt safe! These tears were made up of the pain of years and the terrible need to be loved and cared for.

He didn't make a move to stop her crying, but waited patiently while others gathered and questioned him about the distraught girl. One older woman brought her a cup of water. After she drank it, Mahesh gently guided her back to his house where his wife was waiting with two other leaders from the village. Rhohita sat with the adults and sipped tea that the pastor's wife served her. She looked from kind face to kind face. Then without hesitation, she began blurting out the story that had taken place over the last few days and the conversation she had overheard that morning between the visitors from Kathmandu and the Village Committee Leader and his wife. She was being sold to the visitors from Kathmandu! She started crying again.

The next three hours were a blur to Rhohita. Other Christians were ushered into Mahesh's house and some were given responsibility to comfort her and secure her safety. She was uneasy, but excited, and felt strangely safe all at the same time. Everyone talked as if she was important. She even heard one man say, "God has created her as a woman. She is not to be treated as a water buffalo because of this. What if they come for our daughters?" Rhohita was amazed at the kindness she was receiving from these Christians. These people cared. Why did the high caste people hate them?

Mahesh entered the room again where his wife and two other ladies were protecting her and said, "Little sister, we will see to your safety, stay with my family today." Then he asked the names of Rhohita's brothers and sisters and left.

The rest of this story approaches legendary status in the village areas of Tinpiple and the surrounding Dhading Mountains. Pastor Mahesh and six other men made their way up the mountain to Rhohita's village where they found several people looking for the young girl. The visitors from Kathmandu were sitting in front of the Village Committee Leader's hut waiting for her, seeing that a price had been agreed upon. Their high caste Hindu background gave them a sense of security that was about to be shaken to the core.

In loud, angry voices that rang across the hills with authority, the men from Tinpiple, along with their Pastor, confronted the Committee Leader and the strangers from the big city. The barrage of rebukes and stern warnings that came from

Mahesh drew almost everyone in the village to the commotion. When many from Rhohita's place found out she was being sold, they became angry and outwardly scornful of the Committee Leader. Even if she was low caste, even if she was an orphan, no one had the right to sell her. Not in their village. Mahesh eventually had to step in and plead for calmness hoping to stave off physical harm to the man and woman.

At the end of the confrontation, the Village Committee Leader and his wife fearfully bowed their heads to the floor asking for forgiveness before the whole village and begging the Pastor not to go to the District Headquarters. The visitors from Kathmandu were last seen leaving the village as quickly as possible never to be seen again. A daughter had been saved. Rhohita and her brothers and sisters were to find a new future through the actions of this Pastor and those who gave shelter in their village.

After note: Rhohita and one brother make up two of 30 young orphans who have found refuge through one of the projects supported by The Barnabas Fellowship, Inc. the mother organization of Save the Daughters. Her other siblings were taken to another Christian orphanage. She has a smile that will win you over and does well in school. She told us her favorite subjects are

English and Math, and she dreams of being a nurse one day. When she sings she tilts her head up just a bit and closes her eyes and doesn't hold anything back. That's right! She knows Jesus!!! She sings just like no one is listening but Him. She eats good nutritious food, goes to a good community school, and now has hope. Her eyes now hold a kindness that she gladly shares, and she no longer acts like a low caste girl from the mountains. She will never fear again of being sold for $350 in Calcutta or Mumbai where there would be no hope, no friends, and no family, all innocence gone...in a moment....but...Rhohita is safe.

A Mountain Village, Nepal

The Goat Girl

"Teach a man to fish, and he will fish forever. Find a motivated Nepali girl and give her goat and you'll create massive change." — *Ken Harbour*

Amita stepped lightly from rock to rock as she gingerly picked her way across the small mountain stream careful not to get water on one of the only two dresses she owned. She loved this part of the early morning ritual even when it was raining. But this morning the sun was shining brightly on the rice paddies she had skirted on her way to relieve herself at the edge of the field. The small toilet was all she needed, and she was grateful that she no longer had to squat in the bushes like someone hiding from life.

She paused and bent low letting her hands get clean in the cool water. The sound of the stream making its descent through the ravine and the smells from the neighboring village brought a smile to her face. Life was much better now. And when she was able to smell the rice and lentils cooking from the houses some distance from her hut, it made her happy. She didn't have to remember the dark time.

It had been such a long time since her tranquil life had been invaded by those thoughts that had haunted her like the nagging mosquitoes that found their way into the little village hut at night. You could forget that they were there. Then a sharp sting on the neck or leg would remind you quickly of the tiny attackers always lurking somewhere in the house. A brief chill flooded her mind as she remembered what had happened two days back. One of her goats had gotten close to the big dirt road. It was the small male that had learned to get loose and had wandered from the group. She heard it crying for its mother and immediately dropped her task to go find it. Following the sound, she walked across the fields to retrieve the small, brown and black escapee just as two large lorries rumbled by. They each blared their horns. But it was the stench of the diesel fumes coming from the exhaust pipes that triggered the memories. She would never forget that smell.

In a flash of time quicker than lightening, she was immediately transported back to the dark time when she was a captive in the city with all its horrible pollution and noises and the endless exhaust that climbed slowly up into every possible window crack until it found entrance into your world. She tensed for a moment, but the noise of the water and the sound of the goats asking for their milking brought her back. She relaxed her tight shoulders and took a deep breath looking up at the rising mountains in the distance….yes, life was good now. She had her goats!

She had few friends in the village, but many of them came to buy the goat milk from her now. Some even brought grass and wild beets for her to feed the goats in hope that they would get a discount. She made a special effort to remember those who treated her well, and it soon started paying off. One of the friends she talked to often was Meera. Meera was nearly four years older than Amita who was now nineteen, but Meera had been born with a crippled foot. She would never marry because many thought this meant she was cursed. But Amita knew better. Meera walked with a distinct limp, and many of the young people treated her with contempt as if they were better. The higher caste families wouldn't even look in her direction as they passed. But Amita's smile had won her over and was a welcome retreat from the evil some of the others gave her without cause. Each time their eyes met there was a silent acknowledgement to the universe….we are friends.

There was also her friend old Maya who lived alone since her sons had abandoned her to try to find jobs in Kathmandu. She looked to be 75 years old but wouldn't tell anyone her age. Amita liked to give her small portions of the goat cheese she managed to produce since Maya's teeth weren't so plentiful any longer. This lady had stories that Amita needed to hear, and the kindly words that came from her mouth somehow filled an empty spot in Amita's heart of a mother long forgotten. Then there were the two Christian couples that lived a bit apart from the rest. They had no children, and though they were struggling hard to get their rice crop to grow, they were two of the first families to buy her goat meat when she first started. She didn't understand their religion, but their friendliness was such a welcome change in the painful life she had experienced. Besides, they had that water pump and even allowed her to bring the goats to the pump area. Yes, she liked them very much.

Amita approached the goat stalls she had built and began to talk to her "best friends". There were twenty-four now, and it was all she could do to manage the milking, the curd, and the rambunctious older males. But the constant problems they gave her would change in just a few days she thought. Three of them would be sold for meat and she would have earned more money than many of the other villagers possessed. She thought to herself, "Not bad for an HIV village girl!" Yes, she repeated it aloud, **"Not bad for a HIV village girl!"**

The oldest female goat she had named Lakshmi. She was the best producer, so Amita had named her for the Goddess of wealth. Sometimes it made her nervous to speak to the goat or call her by name since some of the very rigid Hindu people in the village might take offense. But it was what came to her mind so she named her goats with love. She had called the first three goats, received from the foreign organization, names she thought would be pleasing to neighbors, but the village people resented it and chastised her all the more. So each one received the name of a god or goddess or an imaginary friend.

She had set to her task and finished milking the five females when the pains in her stomach started again. It always started as a small ache but grew like the stream during monsoon. Within moments she bent over suddenly losing her morning breakfast. The nausea passed as quickly as it had come. She pulled herself from the side of the tree she was leaning on. It was passing more quickly now than before. When she had first been rescued from the brothel, her fears kept her from expressing anything she was feeling, and her tortured spirit found it nearly impossible to say anything to the people of the international organization that had planned out her successful rescue. All she remembered was that after seven weeks of waiting in a safe-house in Calcutta, she was flown with six other sick girls to

Kathmandu where they had received shots and much interrogation by government officials. All she could think of at the time of questioning was that perhaps if she answered the questions wrong she would be sent back to the place of darkness. She was in as much fear as when she had been trafficked and it had taken weeks for her to learn to sleep again.

When she had finally arrived in the rehabilitation center in Kathmandu, she was treated so kindly. Was it a dream, she thought, as the weeks went by? Would it end? Would the men come in the night? They never did, but a new visitor called sickness was becoming worse. Few wanted to be around her, but several of the other girls who were also infected, had gone through suffering, and a few were much better and were helping the nurses treat the new girls. She quickly learned that not all infected girls survived and that she would have to cooperate with the center to receive the best care. She decided within herself to stand against the rising darkness and be the best patient she could be. That was the first day she made the fist and looked at it as if to say, "I will get better. I will not be a victim any longer." To this day she couldn't imagine where the strength had come from, but after eight months in the rehabilitation facility, she was treated like the rising star. She was helping other girls, encouraging them through their nights of bad dreams as she would sit and whisper words of comfort, or sing little songs when they would shake or cry. She was even asked to help watch over a few of the dying girls as they struggled with their last breath. The understanding that she received from those moments was imprinted deeply on her mind and heart. "Amita," she would say, "you were so lucky to have been rescued." The memory paused as a goat begged for more food. She smiled, yes life was good now. She had her goats.

When the people from the international organization had shown up to ask about girls who were keen enough and willing enough to consider apprenticing in a program that would create a business opportunity for themselves, she had been the first to raise her hand. As a young girl, before the deceptions, in the village schoolroom she was nearly always the first because she knew the answers. This time it was a dream come true. She caught the eyes of two of the people offering the opportunity, and they had scrutinized her with serious looks. She bowed her head like in the dark times. Several days later and after numerous interviews with different people coming to the center, Amita had become one of ten girls chosen for income producing projects....but she would be returning to village life. That was two years ago this month. From the rehab facility, she had been taken daily to the place where the goats were tended. She had spent three months learning everything about goats. She did her best to become the student that would be at the top, and when she realized that the goats brought her so much comfort, it became more than a business opportunity. It became a path of healing for her spirit. For those who gave the goats, the medicine, and the opportunity, it became a life redeemed and a transforming fountain of hope and renewal. For Amita, it was her stepping stone to freedom and self-reliance. She smiled to herself enjoying the thought. A voice outside the goat stall signaled that one of the Christian couples had come to purchase milk. She tied up the young goat and smiled as she came out of her door. These people were so kind! Perhaps she would ask about their God!

Goats are a staple livestock business in Nepal

Danger on the Border

The trip had started at dawn. Esther had gotten up early so that tea would be made for the other members who would come to the front gate soon. Binod was finishing his cold bath. He sat on the stool wiping the excess water from his face and thinking about the soon coming summer and the warm water that would come from the big black tank perched high on top of the house. But the smell of tea and roti, made just the way he liked it, brought him back, so he hurriedly finished and got dressed.

He passed the kitchen on the way to the front door, pausing to look into the living room where Joshi was asleep. He was a valuable team member who had come late last night from a village just at the edge of the Kathmandu valley and stayed the night on the living room floor. Binod gently moved his shoulder, smiling as the older brother murmured something about the floor being too hard for his bones, then Binod left him to take care of personal needs as he finished packing the small car for the trip west. Morning would come too soon, and he must be ready to greet the brothers and see to his family before leaving.

By 6:45 a.m. all the members had arrived. In all, there were six and together they sat in the living room ignoring Joshi's temporary bed now neatly folded in the corner as they broke bread together and sipped tea. Silently they thanked Binod's wife Esther as she brought more tea and even a little warm rice to go with the roti. Binod knew he would have to be quick about saying goodbye to the little ones. His own two children now shared a room with three other orphans from the mountains, but they all called him Buwa (Daddy). This was the toughest part for him. He knew it was tough for two of the other four team members also. Each had responsibilities, wives and children. Two weeks was a long time to be gone. Especially, every month. He could remember when he was little, and his own father would be gone for just a few days. He recalled that it had seemed like an eternity. In his heart, he believed it made him a better father, but he still disliked the leaving.

All the sleeping bags, supplies, and personal items were now in the small Maruti-Suzuki 800. The team began to cram into the tight space each holding something on their lap as older brother Joshi barked orders. They smiled to one another as they feigned acting like little boys hanging on his every instruction. Their manner only made him sterner and the barking orders louder. Little Meera, Binod's youngest at four years, was still clinging to his side refusing to let go. She loved her father so much, and this part always hurt the most. Binod slowly let Esther peel her off. He brushed his hand one more time through his son Amit's hair. As he got into the driver's side, he looked at his wife and their eyes shared the special message which custom didn't allow them to show in front of the other men. That momentary look conveyed volumes. Each knew without a doubt that they would be standing together in prayer. God had given him a wonderful wife!

They left the busy streets of Kathmandu as the fog was lifting. Binod knew he wouldn't see any foreign tourists this morning. It was just too early. Yet it was always a pleasure to see them walking along the busy roadways with their cameras, trying to capture the best picture of something unusual; something that was simply part of Binod's everyday life. He particularly liked the Japanese tourists. They sometimes had two cameras around their necks and like clockwork would get terribly excited about the smallest thing.

For some time during the Maoist party problems, tourism had been cut drastically in the country. This was unfortunate since so many relied on the business. Binod's own brother had a busy shop that sold various souvenirs, and now that the tourists were coming again, the smiles and the rice and dal would be more abundant in many homes.

They made their way up the steep mountainside, twisting and turning at every opportunity to bypass lorries, large trucks, carrying supplies to the west each painted multi-colored and as decorated as the owner could afford. Their precious cargo was everything from cooking oil to rice that would be sold in the cities along the way. He brought a mask to cover his face as dust was becoming a problem this time of year. Binod could hear Bindra and Bhuvan softly singing a Nepali Christian song together, and he smiled, thinking how they hadn't liked each other at first. Now they were brothers in arms.

These outreach trips were some of the best times he'd ever had with other brothers. If ever there was a thing called discipleship, this was it. They shared food, bad sleeping arrangements, cramped spaces, heat, cold, diarrhea and each had learned more about the other than might have ever been learned through casual interchange. They had become very close because they were ministering together. Binod knew they were all respectful of each other's abilities and each had proven a valuable member. No one hesitated to pick up the heavy amplifier that sounded the music and doubled as a PA system in the village, and each had taken pride in the number of villages they had been welcomed into. Binod was amazed at what had been accomplished by the little band of men in such a short time.

He asked Joshi to pull out the map he had made several weeks earlier, and they began to talk about their journey again, knowing that the 500 kilometer trip would take nearly nine hours to make, if there weren't any problems, and if the little Maruti held up. They would travel toward Pokhara, the big tourist town on the Prithvi Highway. That was the busiest road because of all the tourists. It was a major destination for those beginning a trek into the Annapura and white-water rafting had become popular down the Kaligandaki River.

But as they approached Pokhara, they would shunt west on the Mahendra Highway which would take them all the way to the District of Dang Deukhuri. This place had been on his heart ever since he and his counterpart in the United States, had spent several sessions on Skype talking about how to structure the anti-trafficking outreaches. They had arrived at a total of one hundred and seven (107) areas. The leadership knew that they could only go to so many places, so they had spent time in their weekly meetings and individually praying and talking about which ones to choose. Binod hadn't been surprised when Ramesh, the talented guitar player spoke first at one of their meetings and boldly said he thought they should consider Dang. Within moments, each person present seemed to agree. There was some talk about the Chinese border region, but the consensus was to look to the west. They would take their message to Dang.

Now if you were to look at a map of the Dang District Nepal, you'd see a massive road going through the district toward the western cities of Nepalgunj and Rajpur. They are the main routes into India from the west for appliances, trade goods, and other items. But along the border of Dang there were several village district areas that were primarily large hills covered with jungle. Only a few roads went into India from that place. He had decided they would turn south at Chaulahi and travel to the border town of Kolibas. He paused for a few minutes questioning the decision.

It would be rugged, but they had prayed fervently over the area and that was where they felt they were being led. From there they would make their way into rural villages like Bela, which government figures told them had a population of just under 12,000 people. Binod knew they wouldn't be able to visit all 2000 households, but in some of the larger villages, perhaps they could have some impact. It was odd, but after he had spent many hours looking at the map he had purchased in the tourist area, he couldn't help but think that in a place where there wasn't so much government observation, perhaps that would be where traffickers would feel boldest. He had no idea how right he was and what awaited the team.

The first night wasn't good. Mosquitoes! In spite of all the efforts they took to control the stealthy attacks, the second night was even worse. Mosquitoes and more mosquitoes! By the third night, Binod knew he was going to have to spend the day encouraging the team. The main adversaries and relentless nemesis disturbing the evening were the little blood-sucking demons. On the border they went by two names: in Nepali they were "lamkutti" or "kutti" for short, and just across the border less than 15 kilometers away in the Hindi-speaking villages they were called "Macchrom" or Maccha" for short. Regardless of their name, they were just plain blood-sucking demons in Binod's mind and they were nasty. The team had tried to swat as many as they could when they entered the room where they were trying to sleep, but even with the candles burning at all four corners of the room, the little disease-carrying thieves found their way in through every crack and crevice. Each member of the team had accumulated at least two dozen bites and Ramesh wasn't feeling well. Binod wondered if he was coming down with symptoms of

Malaria. He made a mental note, but told the rest of the team, "Watch Ramesh today. Let him carry small items."

Morning found them following the road to a rural village, all in a bad mood as they had spent most of the breakfast time commiserating about nasty insects and beds with little padding. As they stopped the Maruti at the edge of the next village, Binod wondered to himself why had he not thought of mosquito nets? He had heard the history of the area and its infestation with the hard-to-see bloodsuckers, but he had just forgotten. Early in the 1950's and 1960's, few people could live or travel freely in this region. The Tamang people, who had lived there since time began, had developed a natural immunity to the disease, but any unwary traveler would surely find themselves repeating the phrase, "Travel freely in Dang and fever and diarrhea are your companions." There was a massive DDT program by the government to try to eradicate the problem, but Dang itself, being sub-tropical, proved an unwilling partner. "On this trip, we will suffer," Binod spoke openly to the team, but wondered to himself why they had felt such a confidence in coming to this place. Each one tried to raise the others' spirits as they prepared to enter the largest village west of Kolibas. The sun was high, weather was good, but trouble waited.

Stationed at the path that entered the village, Binod noticed, there were just two of them. One was sitting on the edge of a fallen tree, long since forgotten by anyone who mattered. The other stood at the entrance of the banana grove that rimmed the far side of the path. Both wore the latest blue jeans attesting to their status and the smoke that ascended from their cigarettes was blown into the air with a casualness that would make even the worst Hollywood actor laugh. But there they were. As they walked by, Binod noticed the hate-filled glare in the eyes of the big one, the one with the jewelry on. He made a mental note and attached the name "Hater" to it.

Jewelry is important in India and Nepal. And gold is the king of the realm. If you want to show your status, and who among the masses doesn't want to rise just a bit above previously attained rank, you wear gold. If you're a woman, earrings and bracelets are the image-makers. Men get various sorts of rings, bracelets, watches. Anything of this sought-after metal conveys the idea. You couldn't help but see the gleam. The worst example was the gold-rimmed glasses that the second man wore. Yes, they were unique and flashy. Binod thought of him as, "Sunglasses."

But then a third one showed up, stepping out of the darkness between two huts at the end of the village path. There he stood with hands on his hips as if to challenge anyone coming into his circle of dominance. He was even bigger than "Hater" or "Sunglasses", but less concerned about who saw him. He was sure, proud, probably of high caste, and definitely in HIS territory. He must be the leader. He watched with a hidden smirk on his face as the team began their songs and a crowd began to gather. Binod was surprised at the number of people gathering. He thought he'd seen several of them from houses just down the path and then it dawned on him, "They think something is about to happen."

They started the music as normal and the team walked down the dusty paths that separated the houses on either side. Joshi played the guitar while Chandra carried the portable amplifier announcing a special village meeting to help the families. At the same time, they were all singing a popular Nepali patriotic song, but some of the words had been changed to give a very distinct Christian message. After their third trip around the paths they came to rest in the shade of the two large Peepal trees, or Bodhi trees as they are also known. Trees with a religious significance.

Binod did a quick head count, and he roughly figured that nearly 85 people had gathered. But on the outskirts of the crowd leaning on the side of a hut were the ones they had seen when entering into the village: Sunglasses, Hater, and Leader. Strangely enough, two other men joined them, one of whom looked and acted like a high-caste Hindu. The other had an official look about him. He wouldn't meet Binod's eyes. He just let his eyes wander over the crowd.

Binod turned his attention to the youngest member of the team Chandra, who was being trained to share their message also. They had decided to let him take the first meeting as part of the training he was going through. Soon he would be ready to lead a team of his own. As the crowd gathered, Binod could see the fear in Chandra's eyes as the large number of villagers gathered. But it was those sets of menacing eyes focused on him from the back of the crowd that had Chandra worried. Binod walked over to the young brother and took the microphone from his hand while putting his arm around his shoulders and whispering, "Let me take this one….you stand for me in prayer." Chandra gathered the most courageous look he could muster and met the older brother's eyes, but inside he was overwhelmed with thanks that the seasoned leader was going to speak to this large group. He slightly bowed his head and began to earnestly pray over the meeting.

Binod started as usual. He told of the greatness of the country, the beauty of the Nepali people and the worth of every person, man, woman, son, and daughter. But then he started to talk about a great deception that many villagers didn't know about and the "HELL ON EARTH" that awaited any young girl whose parents were deceived by this most heinous lie. He referred to it a number of times as "The Great Deception" that takes away the girls. Now, Binod was a Christian who liked to talk about heaven as much as anything, but he knew Hindus also believed in hell, and it had always gotten the attention of the mothers and fathers standing in the crowds they had talked to. So when he talked about HELL ON EARTH, he spoke with all the conviction and seriousness he could draw from his heart. He would visualize the young girls being sold into the brothels, and when he did this his determination was without limit... He always got the crowd's attention.

He had barely gotten the next sentence out of his mouth when he was interrupted by a voice sounding very authoritative asking for silence. The official-looking man who seemed to be high-caste was no longer at the back of the crowd, but standing before him.

This man was the VDC (Village District Committee) official. He was the chief government official responsible for the village. He wanted to know who gave Binod and his team permission to enter the village and demanded papers giving such permission. Binod greeted him respectfully, but inwardly smiled to himself.

You see, when he and his counterpart in the United States had planned the Save the Daughters outreach activities, they had decided to enlist the permission of the District officials of each area they would be entering. They had started securing permission in the capital of Kathmandu and worked their way to the lower regions. It had never been done before, but as they had secured the legal papers from every district, they realized that the areas they targeted could possibly open up completely to the message of hope. Soon, they found that the teams were invited into the rooms of the main village schools to share with the youth. It was a magnificent strategy, and it was working extraordinarily well. It provided a small blanket of safety, and it had paved the way for so many fruitful outreaches.

Binod handed the man his permission papers after asking the official for his. The man paused and produced his card declaring that he was the Village Committee Chairman and that nothing would take place in the village without his consent. But after looking over the papers Binod had produced, the Chairman grudgingly nodded and stepped back. From the back of the crowd Binod heard a shout, "We don't want Christians here! We are Hindus!" Binod thought for certain it was Sunglasses, but he didn't look up and just continued to answer questions from the villagers about the trafficking of young girls into India.

Soon several arguments had broken out in the crowd. Some were asking to hear the music; some wanted to know more; some were chanting Hindu hymns, and some were jeering the official. Binod looked over the top of the crowd and saw the smiles of victory on the faces of Hater and Sunglasses. Sunglasses took the posture of a victor...speaking into Hater's ear.

As suddenly as the arguments started....they grew silent. An old gentleman who apparently held the respect of many of the villagers had climbed the steps to the top of the wall where the team had set up their outreach signs. He raised his cane above his head and was shouting as loud as his feeble voice would allow a popular nationalistic slogan, "You can take my body out of

Nepal, but you can never take my Soul and Heart from Nepal."
Over and over he repeated it until the crowd became silent.   In a
minute, others joined in and the crowd soon focused their
attention on this elderly man.   A few mouthed words in
admiration of his status.   Hater and Sunglasses just glared with
contempt.   Leader, who thought he owned the territory, had an
unusual look on his face.   A look of seldom-seen concern.

The old man pointed his cane at Binod and started
talking….but not without tears.   "Three years ago," he said in a
voice that quavered with age, "we learned that little Hasina, my
oldest son's daughter, was missing."   He paused and gathered his
strength looking with eyes that held a steel of years gone by.
"She was only 12 years old, but after the family had searched for
days, they came to find out she had been taken to India."   He
choked with tears.   Looking around the crowd, he let his eyes
come to rest on the Village Committee Chairman.   "If these men
had come three years ago, to my son's village and shared this
message, perhaps my granddaughter would be with us today.   So I
will walk with these men to any house in the village that they
want.   I want them to saturate this village so that every little girl
like my little Hasina will never be in danger again.   I will do this
today, even if it is the last thing I do in this life."   Then he threw
down his cane with a force that surprised all.

The crowd was silent....

There was a muttered undercurrent that started to spread across the crowd as the grandfather's words had rescued the moment for the team. Binod looked over at Sunglasses and Hater again. There was a look of confusion they shared as they saw that Leader had strangely vanished. The Village Committee Chairman was talking silently with another man and so Binod took the chance.

He climbed to the top of the steps beside the grandfather and shouted as loud as he could into the microphone so that every house in the area couldn't help but hear him. "You can take my body out of Nepal, but you can never take my Soul and Heart from Nepal! You can take my body out of Nepal, but you can never take my Soul and Heart from Nepal! You can take my body out of Nepal, but you can never take my Soul and Heart from Nepal! But if this is so, why do we even allow our daughters to be taken at all? They are Nepali daughters! They don't belong to India! They don't belong to strange men! They don't belong to the place where there is Hell on Earth! Are there any true Nepali's in the crowd who would honor our daughters? Are there? Are there? Are there?" He kept shouting this without stopping.

But no sooner had he started his chant than the resounding answer came back from nearly every villager....."Hami Nepali! Hami Nepali!" (We are Nepali! We are Nepali!)......."They are our daughters!"........ And the crisis was over.

The team spent almost all day in the village visiting houses. Then they were escorted into two more villages where they were introduced and received the welcome of special guests. They had handed out so many Christian tracts that explained the worth of a daughter, the dangers of trafficking, and the Hell that all believed in, that their supply was almost exhausted.

At the end of the day, they made their way back to the Maruti Suzuki they had left waiting at the first village where they entered and where they now found four men waiting for them. As they approached, one of the men introduced himself and explained that they were also Christians and had been guarding the Maruti. They knew it was late and the circumstances were humble, but they had village friends who wanted to know more about Jesus, and if they would stay the night with them, then hospitality would be offered.

The knot in Binod's throat kept him from speaking for a few moments as he understood the reason why they had felt so led to this place and what an opportunity lay before them that evening. The team was tired and needed rest, and he hated the mosquitoes, but he took one look at the eyes of every member and knew the consensus was unanimous. Even from poor Ramesh who had kept pace all day while not feeling well. With a full heart, Binod answered, "We would be honored to spend the night in this village, Brother. My name is Binod, what's yours?"

Listening intently to an anti-trafficking message

Sitting at Phewa Lake

"When there are people who are equipped and qualified to get a job done, why do we send well intentioned novices from the West to take up the task. Basically, it serves our programs, but their effectiveness of extending the Kingdom is more than questionable." — *Ken Harbour*

It was an absolutely beautiful day and Anil and Suman took their time sipping the hot chai. It was their good fortune to find such a cheap chai stand on this side of town, and the precious liquid that would warm them before their long journey back into the mountains was generously sprinkled with cinnamon and pomegranate seeds. Was there anything on earth like good Nepali tea?

They were sitting at the edge of Phewa Lake, without a doubt the most beautiful lake in all of Nepal. The morning was passing slowly as they waited for the bus to show up that would call them back to reality and their life of hardship in the mountains. Small boats that only the tourists could afford to rent were going back and forth on the lake, many stopping at the restaurant and lodge for a meal. Anil shook his head slowly in a questioning way, but was happy that there were some people there who would make money off of the expensive meals. The world is a funny place he thought to himself. So many had little and some seemed to have all.

They had spent two days walking out of the Lamjung Mountain Range before finding a place where they could ride a night bus into Pokhara. Their families had been left with plenty of rice and lentils to last while they were gone, and Anil had managed to talk one of the poultry farmers out of two chickens. He smiled to himself as he imagined his littlest boy trying to reach for all the chicken when it had been prepared by his wife. Protein was on the menu about twice a month, and his little guy's eyes would light up when he would see that his mother was mixing meat with the rice.

He and Suman had both been invited to the seminar put on by the Western brothers and promised traveling funds and some gifts for attendance. One of the leading Nepali Christians in Pokhara had stressed several times that Anil should attend and Anil knew why. He hadn't wanted the reputation that was afforded him, but here he was stuck with it anyway. Everyone knew of his ventures into the border area of northern Nepal and into China itself. Few had gone and few had cared to go, but he could vividly remember the night seven years ago when he had the dream of Lord Jesus speaking to him. Nothing could stop him after that.

He had been beaten several times in the Buddhist communities, had gone hungry what had seemed days without number, and had even had to sleep in trees several nights when he could find no shelter. He knew better than to be on the ground when the predators came out. But the Lord had been faithful and now there were always the stories among the brothers and sisters about how many new fellowships had been established because of his labor.

Regardless of his desire to not have a reputation, here they were, and after three days of listening to the Western brothers share their ideas about how he should oversee and start churches, he had had enough. It wasn't that he didn't appreciate the fellowship and the passion they had. Their words held the passion so he listened. But most of all he enjoyed the opportunity to see and visit with several of his brother pastors. This was a rare event for any of them, and the time they had enjoyed late into the evening had been rich and heart-warming. He would remember to pray for the Western brothers.

Yet when he found out that the teacher from the West had never started a church in his life, but had only been hired by the church, he wasn't convinced there was anything to learn. Besides, what did they know of his life in the mountains, his people, customs, and needs? They never asked or acted like it was important, but gave them teachings or a workbook they had published. So he just watched and listened trying to understand the motives. In the end, he considered it just a new breed of colonialism, and he was too old for it. They weren't too different from the British who had come years ago. The desire was always to help and the intentions were good, but in the end, they wanted to communicate their superiority rather than understand the people. There were people in the mountains who had requested that he and Suman come share the Good News, and the idea of sitting here another day weighed on his heart. So he told the organizer that he needed to go, and after speaking with Suman late in the evening, they agreed to return to the villages. Now they were on their way home with a brand new bag full of Western material and a gift of $50 for their trouble. He remained grateful for the peace that could be found in Pokhara and the $50. Many of the brothers and sisters from the West who had first come to Pokhara before he was born were held in high esteem. Things were different now.

When he had first started following Jesus, one of the old elders told him of the trials that the small band of Western missionaries had encountered when they first came. The King of Nepal had opened the country up just a bit in the early 1950's and a small band of Western medical missionaries actually walked from India into the Pokhara Valley to erect what would be the first hospital in the west of the country. He paused during another sip of chai tea thinking about the difficulty of that walk. It was sad that so few remained of that type of missionary. His elders had said that these men and women were so in love with the Nepali people. But now, so many came and went that Anil was glad to be in the mountains where, although life was hard, being Nepali still held meaning.

He heard the voice before he saw the man. It was a very distinctive voice, especially when speaking English. He turned his head to the street on his right to see Balram emerge followed by a small number of Western teenaged Christians. He and Suman exchanged quick glances and as they passed by Balram greeted him in the customary fashion, but he quickly averted his eyes from Anil. Suman, his younger traveling companion, was angry that Balram didn't pause to acknowledge Anil. Who did he think he was? Anil was to be highly esteemed!

Suman continued to watch Balram with hawk-like eyes while he walked by and waited for him to at least turn and offer a word of respect to his esteemed brother Anil whom everyone talked about and knew, but this hawker did little but send a word of greeting out of the corner of his mouth. Oh well, here he was playing tour leader again. Everyone in Pokhara knew he would have made a better travel agent, **everyone except the Westerners who came regularly to his church**.

Suman knew the story all too well. Balram had been an orphan with little of anything when the missionary couple from Great Britain hired him to keep the grounds and tend to house duties as a young boy. He was very lucky. No one could doubt that. He had learned to speak English just like the British and as he grew into a young teenager, he was given more and more responsibility. His big break came when the British missionary and his wife were retiring to the U.K. and found a Bible School there that would take him in for his education. First, he would be sent to a good high school in the northern city of Dehradun, India, but then, if successful, he would find a scholarship waiting for him in the U.K.

Suman applied himself and found that his fortunes changed after completing the four year course in the U.K. He returned to Nepal and with his new found skills and connections now had amassed a small fortune by Nepali standards. He had a three-tiered home where he lived with his family. He even had a driver for the 4-wheel drive Toyota that was a gift from the big church in Oklahoma. And yes, he had a gardener and a cook. Balram had built a huge orphanage building and the children had been taken care of well, but everyone knew the property had been put into his and his wife's name. One day it would be used to take care of his family regardless of the orphans. At least once a year he traveled to the U.K. and United States to preach and raise funds for his ministry. Of course, he didn't really have much ministry, but managed to find those who had labored in the rural districts who were willing to be called his pastors as long as a monthly salary showed up on the doorstep. Once a month he purchased food for breakfast to ensure a large crowd at the Sunday service. Yes, Balram had learned well.

Multiple times each year, Balram entertained small mission groups coming to Nepal to help. Anil thought to himself, "They are only here for nine days. What can you do in nine days?" The answer came to him even as he asked the question. He took another sip of tea. Balram had become skilled in helping these eager brothers and sisters from the West "experience" Nepal and that was the way things kept moving, thought Anil. People come, little is accomplished, and the real efforts are rarely helped. He looked into the last of the chai and watched the spices on the bottom of the cup swirl as he moved it around and around in deep thought.

After Balram had moved out of sight with his mission tour group, Suman turned to Anil and asked, "Don't they know anything, Brother? Why doesn't someone tell them?"

Anil hesitated, he didn't want to spoil his traveling companion's opinion of everyone and took his time answering, "Some do, most don't. All are not the same Suman. They differ. They have money, and it makes them feel powerful," he continued. "Do you want more chai?" he asked trying to change the subject. Suman shook his head, but his silence was clearly noticeable.

"But Brother Anil," replied Suman, "there are so many in our place who need just a little to go out in the Name of Jesus. Why don't they understand that we are ready and in the right place? Why seminar after seminar?" Suman paused for a moment then acted as if he was telling Anil a secret. "Respected Brother, I had a conversation with Mr. Sanjay Das who is the government head of the medical system in our district. In private he told me that he gets paid the equivalent of $369 U.S. dollars each month. That seems so much, and you are first person I'm telling. But some of the hotels in this valley are $100 and $200 each night. How much money do these people have? Why can't they help the rural people? Can you even imagine?" he said finishing his tea and returning the cup to its resting place. I think they are so used to living so well, that they don't understand the true way we Nepali people live. They only hear one side of the story that is being given them. It is the way of the visitors. Don't let it become a weight for you. There is much to do.

Anil stood and made sure his pack and extra bag were secure. He felt certain that the bus that would take them into the Lamjung Mountains would arrive any moment. He took a deep breath enjoying the smell of the flowers all along Phewa Lake...proud for that moment that he was Nepali.

"Bhai," he said (the Nepali word for brother), "some do understand. Some take time to learn the language. Some take time to learn about us.   Some, are not proud and full of the denomination teachings they bring from the West, and some, come as servants looking for ways to serve Jesus. All have good thoughts and all have good intentions, but not all have the right instruction. Is it not so among our own people?" He paused as he adjusted his pack and looked with a knowing eye to Suman. People were the same everywhere. They both knew it.

Suman took his time putting his own pack on. He was young, and when he thought of all the times pastors and evangelists in his region had gone without, he wanted to vent his anger. His own family was hungry, while this hawker, Balram, spent all his time taking young people and those seeking a mission experience around the valley sightseeing. But he held his words back knowing Anil would not allow it. Suman made the final adjustments to his pack and hoisted it onto his back. Knowing that no words were necessary, he looked at his older friend anyway and said, "You are right. When they come with an open heart, when they listen to us, live with us, walk with us, and come to know our ministry, then they are different." But his eyes sharpened with a fierceness rarely seen as he faced the older brother and proudly said, "I will never sell myself. I am for my people. My family and I have needs, but I will not sell myself. I am for Jesus!"

Anil smiled inside as he saw the bus come around the corner. But he grimaced as it got closer and he saw that it was already full. It would be a very crowded ride for at least ten hours standing up. But he put his hand on Suman's shoulder and encouraged, "There are those who want to fellowship with us, Brother, and not control our spirits. We will wait until these servants show up. Until then, come, let us go to our families and friends with food to share."

There is power in education, and we love it when the children and women grasp for our tracts and information.

Join Our Cause

So now you've read the stories and have a glimpse into the world of deterring the trafficking of young girls into the brothels of India or other countries. It's the world we think of daily. But the question that is paramount on our minds at this moment in time is, "<u>Will</u> <u>you</u> <u>help</u>?" How many have asked you that in the past, and how many times have you shrugged it off thinking that your gift won't matter.

Well, if that's your mindset right now, let me clear something up. First, in the places where Save the Daughters works and labors, no gift is too small. Honestly, you can change a life with a twenty-dollar bill. Friends of our ministry pool their money to create enough to send a team out for about two weeks into an area we've targeted as having high trafficking activity. The full amount is $1700. Some of our friends are able to give more and a few fund outreaches by themselves. Everyone has the ability to help even a little, but not everyone has the desire. But gifts translate into outreaches.

Here's my second question. If you could stop just one girl from experiencing a brothel where she (even as a 12 or 13-year-old), might have to be serving as many as fifteen to twenty men a day, would you? Would you want to be a part of that opportunity? Could you afford $25 or $50 for that? What if you were the one who gave a young girl hope and a vision that her life mattered as much as anyone else in a society where girls are not valued? What if your gift had eternal consequences?

You can make a difference and know it! This is the goal of our projects. It's not about fruitless activities or raising money. It's about the possibility to create massive change in a life, a family, a village, and a society. It's real. And when you partner with Save the Daughters, your gifts will count. Here's why!

The world is full of busy people. And so it goes in mission and charity work. But in the ministry of THE STEWARD, the person responsible for what has been given them to oversee, it's not about busy as defined by activity, it's about OUTCOME. That's our approach. We are stewards of your gifts. We desire OUTCOME!

The teachings of Jesus are very clear on this subject. "You shall know them by their fruit", He said. This doesn't just apply to the spiritual state of a person, but everything they are and everything they do. More importantly, it's about OUTCOME.

The Scriptures call it "fruit." At Save the Daughters, we are focused on OUTCOME. We want to produce good fruit for you and ourselves in an honorable way that transforms lives and helps extend the Kingdom of our Lord into new places. We are all about OUTCOME. We believe your gifts matter. We want your gifts to have impact and eternal results. Anything else is just religious activity, and we all know there are many organizations and local needs to attract your attention. Our goal is simple, but more importantly, it's effective and it works.

Save the Daughters, is one of the few organizations that will actually address the crime before it happens. We don't wait until a young girl is infected with HIV, suffering from PTSD, and nearly ruined for life by those who would prey on her. We act beforehand. We give them a message of hope that they've never heard before - and we tell them they are special creations designed for possibilities.

Want to make a difference in a world where young girls are preyed upon? Simply go to www.savethedaughters.com and do what you can when you can. Your gift is applied to this project and its needs.

www.savethedaughters.com

About the Author

My wife, Diana and I, both were raised in conservative branches of the Baptist church in West Virginia. She went to college right out of high school to pursue becoming a teacher and I went to Uncle Sam's Air Force. My training in the Air Force was in military intelligence, and with a Top Secret Clearance, I was involved in some pretty serious issues during my tour of duty. Five years later, the Master arranged for Diana and me to meet and in a short time we were husband and wife.

I attended a Christian liberal arts college in Tennessee, and was blessed to see many different types and kinds of Christians. Although I had been raised in a church as a small boy, we stopped going as a family when I was about eleven, and I didn't set foot in one again until a radical about-face at age 22. So at this school there were big Christians, small ones, heavy and thin brethren. There were Presbyterians, Calvinists, liberals, para-church groups, Northern denominations and members of Southern denominations. I was pretty much eclectic and was choosing the best from the lives of the people I could observe. Everything centered on understanding the Scriptures.

As it turned out, I was an Ancient Language/Greek major and spent much of my time in the ancient texts of the Old and New Testaments. After all, that's where truth is found, isn't it? There were few charismatics at this school and those who were didn't make much noise. I guess you'd say they were in the closet.

When it came time to choose a seminary I went north to Indiana to see what all the Northern denominations were about. There were many new denominations and practices which neither Diana nor I had been a part of and the vibrancy of some was incredibly compelling. (*For those remembering the early days of Vineyard, this was the time.*) Again, we weren't part of any charismatic group and the seminary I went to strictly taught the gifts weren't operable today. *(a mistake on their part)*

Diana and I had a desire for missions and particularly to unreached groups. I couldn't see myself making it into a restricted access country in 1980 with a Masters of Divinity Degree so I opted out of Seminary for a new course of service I called "tentmaking." The greater part of the world was closed to conventional mission efforts at that time. For a period of about five years I worked at secular positions always with my heart and prayers in the unreached areas of Asia. In 1985 I was introduced to the concept of "indigenous missions." This was the idea that there were already people in these unreached areas who were native to the culture in their country. Our task was to assist and help them get their task accomplished. <u>Since Motorola, the Fortune 100 Company I was working for, was utilizing the same philosophy</u>, I figured it must work. I mean it was Jesus who said, *"The sons of this age are wiser than the sons of the Kingdom,"* *right?* So with my ancient language background intact, seasoned by a time of learning about business in the corporate world, and a background in military intelligence, I soon found myself and my family living in Charlottesville Va, working and consulting for groups involved in the indigenous missionary movement of the 1980's.

Here's where the real theological education takes place. Scores of leaders of mission agencies from all over the world would come through the Washington, D.C. and Charlottesville, Va area seeking help in raising support for their groups. For a number of years my family and I hosted these leaders from other countries. Many had started hundreds of churches and some were leaders of nationwide movements. They were from Africa, South America, Central Asia, Pakistan, India, the Pacific Rim, and more.

Some had Anglican background, some Baptist, some Brethren, some Church of England and others Pentecostal. The stories we heard of healings and the context of life that people were living convinced us that we hadn't gotten the whole story in Seminary, or Bible School. When you live in a country where there are no antibiotics, no physicians, no healthcare, and it's either the witchdoctor or the preachers, then life gets pretty simple doesn't it? The bottom line is, who has the power! Kind of like Elijah, right?

For over thirty years, my wife Diana and I have rubbed shoulders with believers from many different countries and backgrounds. I've traveled the globe and have had the opportunity to serve with leaders, teachers, and various ministries from many countries. Our service is to the unreached and the disenfranchised Christian minorities. Our goal is to creatively extend the Kingdom of Christ where we can and where others aren't going. We've researched, initiated, and successfully touched the lives of thousands through the various projects we've conducted over the years; they are too numerous to mention here but can be found by inquiry to our ministry. SAVE THE DAUGHTERS, about which this book is written, is one of those projects, and we are proud to have seen such a fruitful ministry develop. We always tell our partners: the right gift, to the right person, at the right time is what makes all the difference. This is our heart...to touch those others ignore. Want to help?

Nothing at all would be accomplished at Save the Daughters without the incredible passion and perseverance that is demonstrated by the outreach teams in the county of Nepal. Their efforts, led by the Nepali Director, have proven to be one of the most successful deterrents to trafficking that exists today. In a given year, these teams will warn, educate, and leave a message of hope with upwards of 25,000 - 30,000 young girls and their families.

Please consider helping us save these young girls

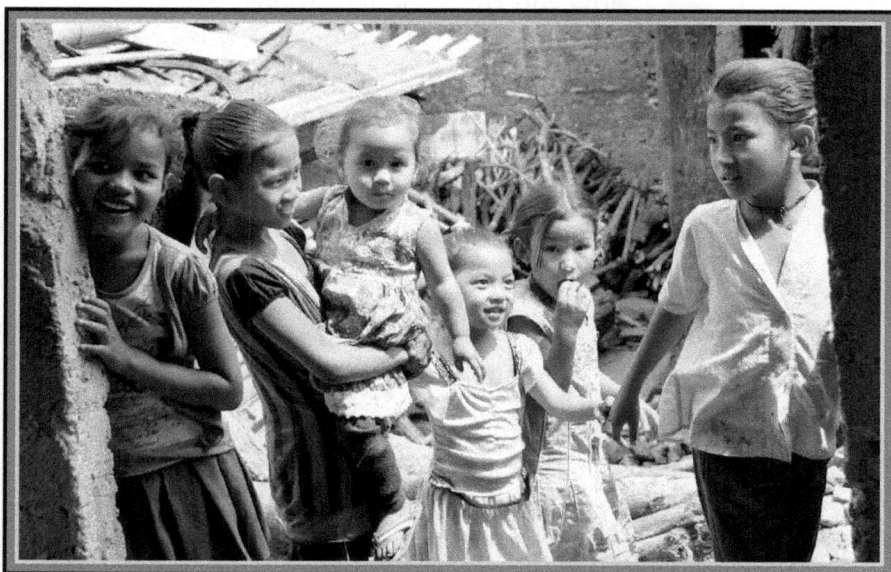

A gift of just $10 a month can make a tremendous difference in the dangerous regions where our teams go.

A gift of $20, $30, or more a month can provide food, tracts, safe places to sleep, medicine, and gasoline.

Our ministry operates by the gifts of people who see what we are accomplishing and who have decided that after young girls are taken, it's too late to get back their youth and their lives.

Why not join us? You've wanted to do something for so long, but didn't know who you could trust or who was actually accomplishing what they say.

Now you know! Join us today.

Donate at www.savethedaughters.com or send your gifts to Save the Daughters, P.O. Box 2398 Forest, Virginia 24551